I0418215

The Ever Changing Business World

The more you learn, the more you'll earn

DOMINIC D'AGOSTINO

The Ever Changing Business World

ISBN 979-8-9861485-4-0   Soft Cover

Copyright © 2022 Dominic D'Agostino

Requests for information should be addressed to:
Curry Brothers Marketing and Publishing Group
P.O. Box 247
Haymarket, VA 20168

All rights reserved. No part of this publication may be reproduced, stored in a retrieval system, or transmitted in any form or by any means, electronic, mechanical, photocopy, recording, or any other, except for brief quotations in printed reviews, without the prior permission of the publisher.

CURRY BROS.
MARKETING + PUBLISHING GROUP

ACKNOWLEDGEMENT

I would like to thank my daughter, Elise and my wife, Rosemary for their work on this book, especially for putting in a lot of time and offering encouragement. I would also like to extend my appreciation to Gina Corbin of GAM for her assistance with the printing of the book.

PREFACE

Before you get into my book, I'm sure you are baffled by the bird on the front cover. The bird represents the title. Business requires keenness and quickness in dealing with business situations in a manner that is likely to lead to a good outcome. If you study birds, their quickness to react, their energy and smartness, those characteristics are just what you need to be successful in business. That is why I put the bird's picture on the front cover of my book. I also in the past have used bird pictures to help motivate workers under my supervision.

Welcome to my second book. The first book, "Strike-Up-The-Band," was about companies in trouble. Knowing they didn't have the proper staffing to get back on track, businesses often asked our company if we could help them. We assembled a team skilled with the proper knowledge, and under our supervision, were capable of putting these companies back on track and into a competitive marketing position.

My major objective with my first book was to give my children a better understanding of why I had to spend so much time away from home. Knowing how quickly they grow up, I wanted them to have some understanding of how companies functioned. Also, knowing the attraction and understanding they had for music, I could explain the similarity between producing a product and creating musical scores. More about this as we go through the book. Now with my children out of school and working, I felt it time to introduce them, and any one with interest, to the many intricacies of business and how you must monitor and adapt their structure to fit the needs of the times. Any of you who have read "Strike-Up-The-Band," have an understanding of the price paid by ill-prepared companies when their present structure could not meet the demands of the post war markets. It was hard to understand how, with their long-time reputations for quality and service, they could fail so quickly and need help from outsiders like us. However, when we got into their modus operandi, it was not difficult to understand. They had done nothing to change their business structure to accommodate many market changes. To meet these demands, these companies attempted to contract with outside producers. However, these outside producers did not match their quality and service. The home companies were now experiencing not only poor quality and late delivery but also over pricing.

Why did I think my children and those of you just entering the business world should know this? Because to have this business knowledge and to feel secure in the business world, you must not only know your job, you must also know the market in which your job functions and understand what the market is doing. We will spend a lot of time discussing the world market and its implications for business. We will also spend considerable time on what had to be done to fix businesses; and, with this knowledge, how to deal with it in the future.

INTRODUCTION

The success of any business and industrial establishment is a function of a wide variety of factors. Some determinants of the organization's successes are not essential to it, whereas others are essential and part of the very fabric of the company. To the extent to which a market is available for the goods and services a firm produces, the availability of raw materials and supplies, and the competitive situation are circumstances outside the organization which play a part in determining whether a company operates at a profit or loss. So we must consider that these factors are largely, though not entirely, beyond the control of the firm. We say not entirely because as executive of the company you have an obligation to monitor these issues and plan accordingly.

There are many essential factors which must be considered so a firm can realize its goals. These factors are essential to the company, and are matters it can do something about such as the structure of the organization, production methods, programs for training and development of personnel and important accounting systems. One of the most important of these essential factors is the talent level of those individuals who manage the firm. The management plots the firm's course and guides its activities. It plays a significant part in the well-being of the members of the firm.

The higher level of managerial talent to be among its executives and administrators, the more effectively the firm will operate, the more adaptable it will be in a changing world, and the longer it will remain in business. It is my hope that the information in this book will give you a better understanding of how good companies operate with awareness of the changing world market. Your success in the business world depends on it.

TABLE OF CONTENTS

WORLD WAR II

    World War II required many quick changes. The upgrading of tools to quickly produce better weapons and the need to replace men going into the service. This next chapter will tell you how it was done and other changes that had to be done.

THE LARGEST MARKET UPHEAVAL IN HISTORY

If you read the Preface, there is a very important sentence that explains those factors a company is responsible for and those that are not. It is the basis for good companies to know how to react to changes that will surely occur. The Preface divides factors into those the company considers to be within or outside their control. This may be true, but the staff members of the company are still responsible for monitoring those factors of the market that they can expect will affect their production cycle and plan and accommodate the changes that must be made to maintain a profitable enterprise.

To give you a complete understanding of one such cycle and how it affected the market, we have to go back to the last century, to the end of World War II. We also have to hope that a large market change like that does not happen again for the same reason. There will always be market changes, and we should always keep that in mind when we are planning. This one was picked because of its size. We can get a good look at what transpired and how it affected the market. The United States had to build an army, and many jobs for the war effort had to be taken over by women. Women were a real benefit to the war effort. To do this, women had to find ways to have their children taken care of. However, when the war was finally over and the men started to come home, the women still liked the idea of the money they were earning along with, now home from the war, what their husbands would be making. Now with more money, they would not only spend on necessities like food and clothing and automobiles, but also for travel, games and many big items they never could afford before. They could even buy two automobiles and new houses. My Dad built houses, and at the end of the war the government was making money available so military personnel coming back from the war could buy homes. My Dad built and sold 32 homes in just one summer.

We must not only consider the essential items that people could now afford, but now they could afford non-essential items. Such items -as games, greeting cards and many other non-essential items were now in high demand.

With the war coming to an end, the United States manufacturing establishment could now shift back to essential home products now in high demand not only at home but could export them to overseas markets. Countries abroad could not produce for themselves for a long time. Much of Europe and Japan was devastated, and so that was another market we would have until they could rebuild their countries. We now had airplanes, the United States developed for the war effort, that could fly products to anywhere in the world.

Many businesses failed to see this big market change on the home front. When the store owners first saw the demands for new items or even old items now selling that were in the store for a long time, they were very happy. However, when they could no longer meet the demands and had to put up with outraged customers, it was no longer fun. They would badger the suppliers until the suppliers had to find other means. The suppliers started to turn to outside producers to help fill the gaps.

Many of these outside producers were late with deliveries of poor quality. This is an important situation that we must spend considerable time on because adapting to market changes effectively is very important to the success of a company. The next chapter will give you the answers on to how to handle changes that must be made in a company structure to address market changes.

EXPLORATION IN MANAGERIAL TALENT

When you think about the changes in the markets during World War II, you have first to go back to the war years to understand the changes that needed to be made to produce the goods and services to support the war effort. The expansion of these plant facilities required not only more labor and equipment but an expansion of the managerial staff as well. There was also a demand for more products and with improved quality and with upgraded functional capabilities. All these changes required an upgrading of managerial personnel as well. The acceptable management just before the war would no longer suffice to face the new world order.

The companies involved with the war effort had to adjust to the new world effort quickly. So they made the effort to school and train their managerial staff to fit the many new changes needed in the war effort. Those companies that were in the civilian market did not have the war market explosion of the same magnitude. Theirs came much later with the worldwide civilian recovery. They were ill-prepared to handle the overwhelming production requirements demanded by the new market size. Companies not having the skilled staff to monitor the purchasing of finished products from outside sources for price, quality and on-time delivery were getting costly rejections and losing valuable customers. Their two-tiered company, made up of top management and in-house production, was not adequate to handle the new market. They had very little, if any, experience in purchasing finished products from outside producers. To correct this, a third-tier had to be added. This tier would be made up of personnel experienced in outside purchasing of finished product. In order for these two-tiered companies to speed up the processes, they had to contract with companies that had personnel with three-tier experience. They would use these companies' personnel to act as a third tier.

These three-tier companies would also train new employees to add a third tier to the companies lacking the knowledge in outside purchasing of finished product.

If you have any real interest in how some companies handle this market surge, my first book, *"Strike-Up-The-Band"*, goes into depth on how we successfully restored five very respected companies before the war that had poorly prepared for the "market surge" and who were for years, before the war, well known for their quality and service. They were now in the market surge failing in product quality, service, and also losing money. We restored these companies in a very short time and put them back on a path to recovery. There was no end to the thanks we got from them when we finished our assignments. Companies should always be vigilant of their market acumen as this book states.

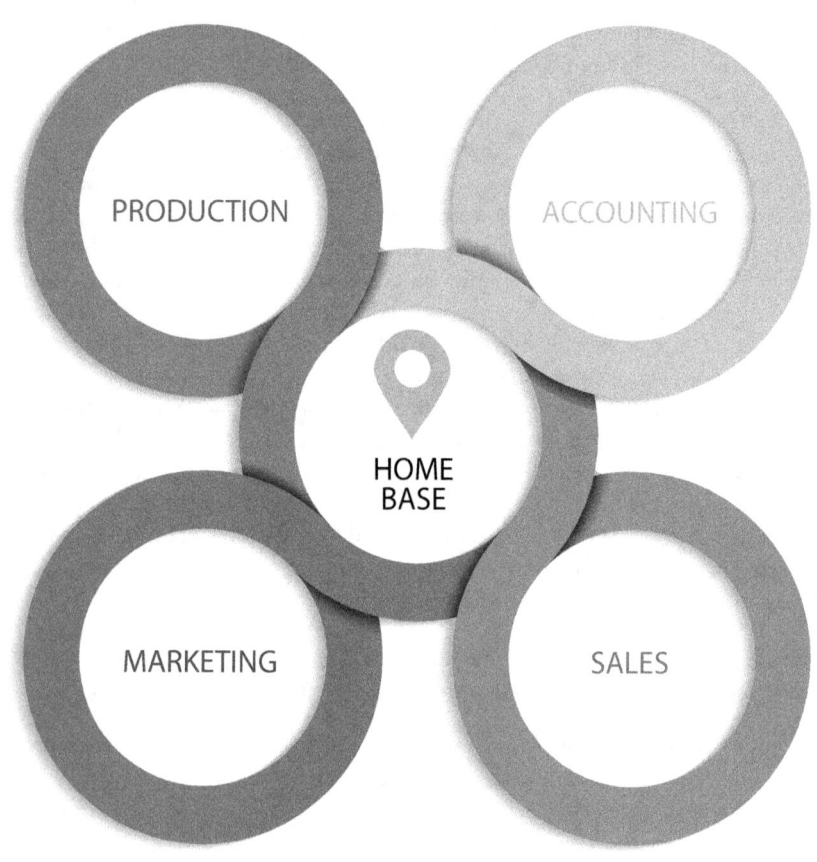

PRODUCTION

ACCOUNTING

HOME
BASE

MARKETING

SALES

Working teams have become spread out and smaller, requiring more leaders than before. This has become a problem finding employees with leadership abilities.

BUSINESS ACUMEN

Well, here we are again, seventy years later discussing changes that affect our way of running a business. As you read in an earlier chapter before this one, it was all because of World War II that we had to find new and quicker ways to conduct our businesses. Now, seventy years later, we are finding out that technology has forced us to again change our methods of doing business. Business acumen is no exception.

For many years business acumen was for a few top management position members of a company. They were considered the decision makers for their team. They were expected to have knowledge of the project and how the team would work to make the right decisions. It was expected that the project would be successful. These top-of-the-line managers were expected to have business acumen. The use of the term acumen we know means that they would make good decisions and that the outcome would be successful. This program and company structure worked very well for years. However, things started to change as we all know. Companies have gotten so much bigger and spread out in different locations. Working teams have become smaller and spread out. Each team must have a leader. Because of this new setup, there must be more leaders available. Many companies that now service wide areas cannot find employees to fill these leadership positions. Why this shortage? It is understood that 80% of the employees in these companies do not have the basic literacy of their business or strong enough business acumen to fill these jobs.

Companies now find they must invest in business acumen to develop personnel to fill vacant jobs, but find it difficult. You also know that to do your job you need knowledge of what the job entails. Study the budget, the number of employees that are needed, what this all will cost. Learn as much as you can about the company you work for. Read company reports if their available. Follow up with anything that gives you all indications of the market you are in. Money people, customers, innovation, products, service offerings are all important to understand and comprehend.

Once you have gained the knowledge, you are ready for developing acumen. This will not be easy, but you must count on the knowledge you have acquired to help you make the decisions. The decision should be a calculated one, not reckless and you may not always succeed but you must always try. Acumen will always have an element of risk attached.

As a final note, business acumen is keenness and quickness in understanding and dealing with a situation in a manner that is likely to lead to a good outcome.

OPEN FOR BUSINESS

Strength, Weakness, Opportunities & Threats

ENTREPRENEURSHIP

A person with a good business sense should be able to retain essential information and focus on key objectives. He must also be able to recognize the options available for solving problems and then select the right approach to overcome those obstacles. As an entrepreneur, he must be able to set in motion a plan that gets things done.

To be a successful entrepreneur, you must be self- motivated. You must also know what is offered and how it fits into the market. You must also take well thought out risks which include using basic money management skills and knowledge of the process. Another great deal in your success will include flexibility and passion because starting a business can be daunting. However, many people open successful businesses each year. Those who do succeed typically spend significant time raising capital, doing marketing research and developing a realistic business plan before launching their new company. Of course, careful preparation isn't an absolute guarantee of success, but it can improve your chances enormously. Take stock of your resources and be prepared to meet the many challenges you will encounter.

Those who are just starting out in business or who have an existing business, including sole proprietors, general partners, limited liability company members, and even corporations, should have a business plan to map out their strategies and goals for the company. A business plan is essentially a tool for planning and education. It can also be used to build the framework for your enterprise and set goals for the business. It can also be used by start-ups as a way to present ideas, sales projections and plans for achieving your objectives to potential investors for funding purposes.

Ultimately, whether you plan to launch a company, transition from being a freelancer to a small business owner, or wish to recreate, improve, and organize your current business, a business plan is a helpful document for steering your business forward and informing others of your plans. Your business plan should include important sections. The first may be an "Executive Summary." This portion of the plan summarizes your company. It should include an overview of your company's management structure, a prescription of your product or service, your goals, and analysis of your finances and marketing strategy. It should also include if you have one, a brief rundown of your business history, ownership, and its mission or vision statement. Here you can also include a breakdown of what your product or service is and its unique features, and patents if you have some, as well as any future products you may want to develop.

An important part of this analysis is your competition and how you intend to compete against them and their strategies. A SWOT analysis consists of "Strengths, Weakness, Opportunities, and Threats." A SWOT analysis evaluates these specific aspects of your business.

An operation overview is very important to be done periodically. It provides a glimpse into the daily operation of your business, including the management and staffing, structure, human resources plan, your physical operational facility and production methods, such as quotas or manufacturing details. It should also encompass your capital requirements. You should update this plan whenever situations change that you feel a need for changes in your plan.

To be a successful entrepreneur you will work harder, longer, and better than anyone in your company. But at the end it will all have been worth it.

INNOVATION IS KEY

"To begin or introduce something new is to innovate, but innovation is the act of doing something newly introduced."

I know very few businessmen who have not been innovative. I'm not only talking about the ones we read books about or read in the paper. I'm talking about the everyday leaders, or businessmen, who developed new ways of doing things which will make the job safer or better or save money. In reality, I can't think of anyone who is an outstanding leader or successful business owner who is not innovative. Innovation is a must for every company. Companies expand growth by creating new products and services. However, it is important to know your limitations. Some companies only think of blockbuster ideas that will result in big profits. This is not the best strategy and could be very costly to the company. Better to think of small ideas that could generate real profitability. You must also keep in mind if you deviate from your present business plan there may be need for you to make changes in both your production and marketing procedures.

This was true in my business twice, once when we took on a target printing business and another time when we got involved with a publishing business. In each case, we were very successful in making the necessary changes in both production and marketing.

The major factor in being innovative is to never accept a bad situation as it is, but find a better solution. There will be times when you think you cannot win. However, if you stop trying you will never win.

You have to look at a business venture like a plant growing. If a plant stops growing, it is going to die. The same thing happens to a business. You must keep it growing, and you do this mostly by innovation. You find new markets and better ways to produce your product or even a better product for a new market. For those of you who have not read my first book, *"Strike-Up-The-Band,"* it has proof of this concept.

In the first print shop I purchased, the two printers who owned it were also interested in fire arms and belonged to a club that used a local range. Being printers, the range owner asked them if they could print targets. They said they could, but the small size of their printing presses would limit the size of the targets they could print. The range owners were alright with the size. The policemen, who used them, only shot at small bullseye targets, as most police personnel did at that time. When I took the company over, I continued to market the targets to police force personnel wherever I could. We did other printing as well for local companies and stores, and the printing business was growing. We were building a good operation, and we had moved to a larger space and put in larger presses. The target business felt like a sure thing for me. When I purchased the printing company, I also made sure of my ownership of the target business it was doing. The name of the target business was Speedwell Targets. I ran both the printing business and the target business, but later put Speedwell Targets in its own company with me as the only partner. I spent considerable time working on getting it going. Now with the larger presses, we could manufacture larger targets. At a gun show in Atlanta, we passed out free targets to the people who were there and got a great response. We also talked to as many police officers we could find there about no longer shooting at "Bulls Eye" targets for practice but at the newly produced "Thug Target" and the center of mass. The trip to Atlanta got me more enthused with the target business, and so I decided to spend more time on it. My daughter Elise was home from school for her summer break, and I put her to work going through state records to find the names and addresses of many law enforcement agencies in the United States she could find. We then put out four 800-number telephone lines. We hired actors in their off hours from the New York theater district. We used them to call law enforcement agencies and tell them about our targets. We had our marketing staff write the script. The actors then went country wide over the phone lines and did a very good job presenting our target products. The target marketing program was a great success. We did very well with the target business for many years, and at which time I decided to sell out and retire.

Since I retired and sold my target company some twenty years ago, it has become the largest target company in the country.

However, retirement was not to be. I received a call from a company that I had done work for with my printing company, and we had become very friendly. They were in advertising and needed some help in managing art and printing production for customers. I offered to go to work for them to see if I could help them out. One day the marketing company got a call from one of their customers. Their customer wanted to know if they could help with production problems they were having from outside producers. Now, if you have been reading my book, you will already know about production problems and why they were happening. The marketing company I was now working with already knew who could help their customer out. I was called in to see if I would go to help them. We talked about the assignment and settled on what my new compensation would be. I went out to the distressed company to find out what we could do to help them. I came back to the office and put together a team of players to help solve their production needs. This was just the start. We built a reputation and spent the next few years fixing distressed companies. Mostly all were suffering from the same illness, poor business management by not knowing how to innovate.

LEADERSHIP

"Leadership is the capacity to direct and guide the effects and actions of others"
(Author Unknown)

Let's get one thing out of the way. Don't believe what you often hear about leaders only being born not created. Leadership capability can be acquired through knowledge, understanding, and dedication. Now with the understanding out of the way, we can get on with what leadership really is and that is at the top of the page. How you become a leader is as follows:

You must start out being the best member of the team you can be. You must be resourceful and a team player. Your thoughts should not be on leadership but on getting the job at hand completed. You must be a team player and also be respected by your other team members. You should have genuine interest in the job you are doing. Knowledge is power, and you will find many opportunities to use the knowledge you acquired. Many times conditions on the job demand quick attention, and your knowledge and alertness will be noticed.

Be helpful and understanding to the members of the team. It is important that you are liked. If and when you do become a team leader, you will find that if those under your supervision like you, they will produce better for you. In this first leadership position, you usually will have to count on the respect you gained when working with your fellow workers. You will not have much prestige in your first leadership position. All eyes will be on you and how you react to being in this new assignment. A safe rule will be to treat subordinates in a way that you would want to be treated. Management will also take notice of how your fellow workers react to your new leadership role. When the dust finally settles, how your department performs will be the final test of your competency. The members of your team will work with you because they, more than likely, know you and know their job and what is required of them. However, after they work with you for some time and you treat them fairly, you develop their trust. If you build the right relationships, they will follow your instructions. You will find that doing a good leadership job does not go unnoticed by companies who are growing. You must also continue to grow in leadership ability, and most importantly in the knowledge of how the company you are working for operates.

The qualities you are trying to instill in your team are the qualities you must possess and model. Besides motivation and communicating effectively, you must also be vigilant in understanding your teams needs, so they can function at their full potential. Only after that do you consider your own needs so that you continue to set a good example.

Other important qualities of leadership you don't hear mentioned very often are vision, creativity, and anticipation. Here again, we are looking at skills that, with some effort, can be developed. No matter the position of your team in a situation, you have to be looking ahead. Through knowledge and experience you should acquire the ability to anticipate the most likely places for problems to occur. Having this information in advance , will allow you time to visualize the problem and use your creative skills to either develop alternate plans or seek advice.

Your leadership does not stop with production. Companies need both sales and production to be successful. Companies need to grow to remain profitable. You must also continue to grow and gain knowledge and understanding about the company. As the company continues to grow, they will need more leaders to do that, and they will expect you to help with that. You should also encourage those under your supervision who have leadership potential to work towards that goal. Also, there is only one way for you to move up and that is if there is a reliable replacement for your current job.

I will not bore you with my path through the many companies that I worked for. I will tell you that these principles work, sometimes business failures are the fault of those in seniority above you, which you have no control over and that you will have to contend with. There may be members of the staff, for one reason or another, who will not be happy about your moving up through the ranks. Politics exists even in plant management, and you will have to learn how to handle it. Try to build relationships with other members of the company when you can, like members in sales or purchasing. When I was let go from a company while I was a plant manager and had already been acting as regional manager for four of their other plants, my reputation was well known by other companies in the business. I got a job within days after being let go by the first company. I was hired as plant manager, and after a few years, they started to talk to me about who could take my place so I could move up. Not wanting to play this game any longer, I formed my own printing company with some partners. However, I still maintained the decorum I learned through the years I spent becoming a leader.

Before I close on leadership, I want to leave you with one more important item that has come to my attention. I think, from my experiences, that it is important enough that you should consider it in your daily routine when appropriate. A study has been done that confirms that when possible, instructions should be given in writing. This issue has recently been raised, and I feel that it should be considered whenever you are issuing important instructions to your team. The thinking behind this is that in the writing of the instructions, you will give more thought to it, and it will be more exacting in what must be accomplished. It will also help those carrying out the assignment as a means of checking that the task was fully carried out. To handle assignments in this manner may require more thought and time, but it should provide much better results. It will be interesting to see how popular this procedure becomes in the future.

I would like one final note on this subject. Having spent years in leadership, I can't remember how many times I have given instructions on a project orally, and many of the instructions were forgotten or not fully carried out. To help you with this exercise, if you chose to use it, here are a few guide lines to follow. Consider using a header for each procedure and a numbered heading entry for each step. Use complete sentences in each step. Close your guide lines with your need for a report when the project is complete. This should be of real interest in how well the procedure catches on.

BUSINESS AND THE IMPORTANCE OF RELATIONSHIPS

You will find it very difficult to be successful without the ability to develop meaningful relationships in life as well as in business. At this point, you might be thinking, "This is all well and good, but I'm not a people person." Just remember that the ability to build relationships, like leadership, can be acquired. The effort must be made. Going it on your own will not do it. You must build a group of players who will support your efforts as you build your career. Remember, it is important that real relationships are built not only on what you want, but also about what others in the group want. In fact in their book, Mark Coulston and John Ullmen wrote, "This isn't something you can achieve by manipulating people. In fact in an age of social networking, the negative influence generated by insincere tactics and trickery can destroy your relationship and reputation in a heartbeat." Of course, this is also true in business relationships.

Years ago the book to read about relationships was Dale Carnegie's *"How to Win Friends and Influence People."* However, in this day and age, the book by Mark Coulston and John Ullmen, *"Real Influence"* is more in tune with today's world. This book is not just about getting what you want, but about forming strong relationships by understanding each other's viewpoints. This is important reading for entrepreneurs.

Being in your own business, you can sometimes feel very lonely when wrestling with a problem, one that you can't discuss with any of your employees because of its sensitive nature. That is when it's great to have a network in place that you can go to for advice and understanding. You can put this network together yourself or look for existing peer groups you might be able to join.

These groups come in many different forms. Some are established by a product, others by location. Those that have the same product may not serve the same geographic area. Those that are from the same geographic area may market different products and services. There are many benefits for joining one of these groups. They can help you expand your market by introducing you to new customers. If you are in a peer group producing the same products, there may be opportunities in bulk purchasing. These are just a few of the benefits besides the knowledge you will gain from sharing information. As I stated in the beginning, you will need to be a contributor in relationships, and peer groups are no exception.

For many years, I was on both sides of such encounters, and they are rewarding in either case. In networking, you may not only get help with a problem but also find opportunities to influence others in the group. I remember with the target business we would want all of our competitors to know we raised our prices. They would judge this news as a good time to maybe consider raising theirs. Many of my business relationships became solid friendships and still exist today. We may not get together or talk often, but when we do, the conversations are like we talked or got together yesterday. Even though we may no longer be in a business relationship, we still respect each other's knowledge and honest judgment. There are times when you are just looking for verification. In these present times, we can't always trust the information we are getting.

Through the years, many relationships have expanded to include spouses and children and are now more social like weddings, graduations, clubs, and such. I'm sure you have all heard it often growing up that you are known for the company you keep. This goes for the business world as well. To be recognized as part of a successful business group can have a real influence on your business.

I was never made more aware of the importance of relationships then when I was invited by a business friend to hear Harvey Mackey talk about his book on business relationships. I of course agreed to go. His book is *"Swim With The Sharks, Without Being Eaten Alive."* This is required if you ever want to get ahead of the pack.

The friend who invited me, Bill Horne, and I had dinner close to where Harvey Mackey would be speaking. After dinner, we got to the auditorium a little early and watched as over a thousand seats filled up before Harvey made his entrance. He started his lecture talking about how he built his envelope manufacturing business into one of the largest in the country. He was a name dropper, and the list of names he felt he had strong relationships with was very impressive. When you read his book, note the number of endorsements from people from all walks of life preceding his text. He talked about deals that were made possible only because of his contacts. He spoke over an hour; he spoke about the importance of relationships and negotiating skills and then took questions. One comment he made sticks in my head, "Everyone by the age of 40 and healthy should have a rolodex filled with contacts they can talk to as if they talked to each other every day." You must remember this was way before computers and cell phones, but the basic idea remains. Even though I am on the computer daily, the rolodex still sits on my desk at the ready.

A lot goes into relationships—common interests, accountability, truthfulness, and much more. Always remember a healthy relationship is a two-way street. If you are a user without being a provider, over a matter of time, you will be found out and on the outside looking in. You will only get out of relationships what you are willing to put in. This is especially true in business relationships. I believe through the years, even before hearing Harvey Mackey's lecture, I did a fairly good job building relationships, but after his lecture, I became even more aware of its importance. After the age of forty, I never wrote a resume'. Every assignment I had after that age was from relationships I had nurtured.

I was always mindful of the responsibility that came with being recommended for an assignment. Not only is your reputation on the line, but so is the reputation of the individual who recommended you. Do everything in your power to complete the assignment to the best of your ability. It is important that you also find ways to thank those who recommended you. I still enjoy meeting new people and talking shop. I can't help it; it's in my blood. I have found that nowhere is developing relationships more important than in small family businesses. After they get to know me, they discuss freely their business operation. Some problems they understand but do very little to correct. Others they are not aware of will become major problems in the future. Most of them survive because the glue that holds them together and functioning is the patriarch; and, until his retirement or demise, these underlying problems will not be fully addressed. I have had discussions with family business owners, and even though they know that these issues exist, they never seem to find the right time to solve them. Family business relationships are very complex because they contain elements such as love, dependency, attachment, intervention by other members and so much more. Most family business patriarchs struggle with succession plans because they fear the repercussions. They fail to realize that every situation or problem solves itself, but not always to your liking.

Some of the family business issues I have had a front-row seat to because I had an on-going business relationship or a relationship with the family. Some I was asked to help in the decision making process; others I was called in to help solve the business problems that developed in the transition. The heart breakers are the ones where the patriarch is the sole owner, and his children worked in the company for years. He decides to sell the company at retirement age, and his kids are told they will still have jobs.

There were family companies where a son-in-law came into the company. Not having grown up as a member of a family-owned business, he went to college and received a good education. The family members may have also gone to college, but they did not put in any effort because they were going into the family business. Now who is better qualified to run the family business?

One problem that keeps recurring is what I call the "full cash register." The company ends up in the hands of the son or daughter. At some point, I am called in because the company is now in trouble. They can't understand it. The company did so well when their parents ran it. When they needed money, their parents would say, "Take it out of the cash register." There was always money in the register. They never once thought how that money got there. Their parents worked twelve-hour days and watched every penny that was spent. They now are in charge and work eight hours or less, have no idea of how much they spend, with too many employees and not enough customers.

I had one good discussion with an owner of a family business that made a lot of sense. He would have his children find jobs in other companies first. They would have to be successful in their jobs for three years and then could make up their minds whether they wanted to come into the family business or not.

CHANGE FROM GOOD TO BETTER

Technology Leads the Way

CHANGE FROM GOOD TO BETTER

For a company to stay in business today, it must always be changing. It must not only go from bad to good, it must also go from good to better. Change is necessary for a company that is number one to stay as number one. There are many prime examples on this subject.

The auto industry in the United States back in 1970 was the world's major producer of automobiles. They assumed that the world wanted big cars, and because of that, they would retain 85% to 90% of the world market forever. Well we all know now how that worked out. The markets changed to smaller cars and of better quality. Most of the auto companies in the United States were ill prepared for it. So this is the first lesson about change. Incorporate flexibility into your production process so you can react quickly to change. After what happened in the 1970's, Ford studied how Japanese companies like Nissan handled production and inventory control and changed their methods to match. Ford 2008 needed no bailout. General Motors and Chrysler both needed help from the government to stay in business.

We have the best military in the world. To make sure we keep that position, we have one branch developing new weapons and another branch developing ways to defend against them. The military constantly updates training methods to make sure they stay the best.

We keep talking about change being difficult. The difficulty is most prevalent in large successful companies. The reason for this is because few employees rarely participate. Most feel they have been doing a good job and don't have to get any better. Also the participation can be improved by the way the change program is presented.

Some companies hire outside consultants to take the team through a "Behavioral Change Technology" program. These programs have no specific improvement agenda. In the interest of training as many employees as they can in the shortest possible time makes it an academic experience. If with the diverse group a particular project were to be discussed, most times the knowledge necessary for all to participate is lacking. Those who know little about the project being discussed or feel they have no desire to participate lose interest in the program. The idea was that with this training, an employee would now go through their assigned area of responsibility and take the initiative to make improvements. It has been my experience that this rarely happens. *Best Practices* is such a training program.

I have found it more productive to work with a small group of employees who are familiar with the production procedure and have a stake in the outcome. I try very hard to make the necessary changes come out of their mouths. Sometimes, this takes a little time, but it gets them committed to the outcome. We used this principle very successfully in a rejuvenation project I led for Sky Box, a company that prints and distributes trading cards.

Change does not always have to be dramatic to be successful. Sometimes a minor change can produce a major improvement. When I was with the first check printing company, the bindery supervisor and I were unhappy with the proofreading department. Poor proofreading of the finished product leads to costs for reprinting and additional costs for packing, handling and postage. An even bigger problem is the customer's lost time in having to wait for a reorder to be produced.

I spent some time observing the proofreading operation, which was an open area to the rest of the plant and right next to the binding operation. The proofreaders sat on high stools overlooking the rest of the plant. Any slight disruption in the plant, you would see their heads pop up. Now you understand that they must look up occasionally to give their eyes a rest. However, these constant disruptions were not good. Behind their work area was a windowed wall. At the end of the shift, I had maintenance turn desks around to face the windows. When they looked up now, they had a view of the industrial park. Proofreading improved, but I might add that, in some cases, just your interest in trying to solve a problem and talking it over with the department, results in improvement. I have seen it happen with just painting walls or better lighting.

One major reason for change is to make product improvements. These improvements could have any number of quality objectives: such as, lower sales price, better performance, longer life, etc. Successful companies are built on quality products. Quality was always foremost on my mind when developing a production process. One day sitting in a chair having some dental work done, I spotted a plaque on the wall in front of me. I thought it was the best definition of quality I had ever seen.

"Quality is never an accident: it is always the result of high intentions, sincere effort, intelligent direction and skillful execution: it represents a wise choice of many alternatives."

MAKING MAJOR NECESSARY CHANGES

The basic goal for making changes is to keep up with the challenging market environment. The most general lesson to be learned, from the more successful cases, is that the change process goes through a series of phases that in total usually require money and a considerable length of time. Skipping steps creates only the illusion of speed and never produces satisfying results. A second very general lesson is that critical mistakes in any of the phases can have a devastating impact, slowing momentum and negating hard-won gains. Most of us have very little experience in organizational changes. It is important that everyone involved is in favor of the changes and will make every effort to make it successful. Without motivation, members of the team will not help, and the effort will go nowhere. It is hard to drive members of the team out of their comfort zones. They worry about all the things that could go wrong. This is when you need good leadership. Everyone must know the changes are a necessity to build the company up to a new level, and that everyone will benefit from its success. Every member involved has a good picture of what the company is changing to and the benefits it will bring to all in the company.

Changes in a company are inevitable. A company must be looking for growth, and this can only come about with change, for example, better and bigger equipment such as in our case, better and bigger printing presses. We started with two small letter presses and over the years went to larger offset presses. We also expanded to add other equipment to handle all of the ancillary printing and finishing equipment needed to produce the printing programs we were contracting.

The changes did not stop at equipment. As we expanded, we outgrew the floor space we needed. This required our moving to larger space in a new location. This became a problem with some employees, and we had to settle this with the printers union. We kept are minds on the positive growth pattern we were on and with confidence that the union matter over expanding our facility could somehow be settled.

The changes over the years were astronomical. We had gone from a small letterpress shop to a four color offset printing plant producing four-color book jackets and book covers for leading book publishing companies and shooting targets for law enforcement agencies and the USA government.

Whenever we needed to make a change, we always kept it in a "yes we can" environment. When you do it as many times as we did, your employees get to know you will get it done, and how it will benefit everyone in the company. This is important because you need everyone in the company to make the change work. It is in everyone's best interest.

THE HAND-OFF DETERMINES SUCCESS

Employee Honesty and Integrity
Each department must pass the job on to the best of their ability.
The Stop Watch Concept; One thing stops, the project is stopped.

EMPLOYEE HONESTY AND INTEGRITY

It is important, no matter the size of the company, to have a code of ethics and professional conduct book available for employees. You may think your company, because of its size does not need it. I can tell you from past experiences your employees have to know the seriousness of not following employee guidelines at work. The book does not have to be elaborate. However, it should provide a good understanding of what is expected of employee's work ethics while on the job. You can put your own book together that would be specific to your company needs or check in book stores as to what is available.

In the years I was leading my printing and target business, I attended many business outings. There, I would meet owners from large and small companies. Most of them knew me, because I either helped them with a print production problem or other problems they were having. One of the big problems that would always come up was about employees and the problems they were having finding good talent. The problems would range from costly errors of judgement to forgetfulness and up to deliberate and costly acts. Many times the business owner or company official I was talking to was more offended by what happened because of the trusted relationship he thought he had with the offender. One major reason for this honesty or integrity problem to exist in a company is because you don't make it a serious enough issue in the managing of your company. Your employees must know from the first day they start work in your company that you are serious about trust but verify in everything the company does.

Your participation in the action of your company will give you a good indication of your strengths and weaknesses. You will also be aware of what the customers most want from your service like higher quality or faster service. Your participation in the operation of the business will help you in the direction if there is a need for money and product to be exchanged then make sure that records and member names are recorded on the transaction papers and verified that the transaction was completed and recorded properly. There is much more you can do on this subject that will help improve both honesty and integrity. Demand an orderly arrangement and neatness of your facility. Any company not being orderly is an invitation to help yourself to whatever you want without proper authorization. The most prevalent is the stockroom. Good record keeping should be mandatory, and keep it closed or at least not easy to be in without being noticed. Any material coming out of the stock room should be recorded.

On this subject I am reminded of President Ronald Reagan. "Trust But Verify" was one of his favorite themes. While negotiating a treaty with the Soviet Union in 1987, he mentioned it so many times that Mikhail Gorbachev complained. A few years later, Soviet colonels in full dress uniform watched as USA B52's and ICBMs were chopped into little pieces, while American Colonels watched the same procedures on Russian Bear Bombers and their ICBMs. It was one thing to say they destroyed a Nuclear Weapons System, and entirely another to see it destroyed. Owners of companies must adopt the same standard. Blind Trust can be abused. A prudent verification process is essential. Even more important if a trust is violated, punishment must be evaluated and justly served.

MARKETING

The first thing is to know your business. Stay in touch with production for quality and on time delivery of product and service. Staying in touch with the operation of your business also will keep you in touch with your customers. You will also gain important information that can help you expand your company and be more successful. You will do this by analyzing your strengths, weaknesses and threats. Your reputation is most important in making and keeping your business profitable and successful.

A very important part that is necessary for you to always keep in mind if you want your company to prosper and grow. You should always be looking for opportunities for your company to grow. Remember the chapter on Innovation Is Key. No matter what business you are in, it will always be changing and you must stay aware of it.

On a personal note, if while you were reading the book you may remember when I first bought my printing company, I knew nothing about it having a target operation as small as it was. Over the years, when I got into marketing the target business and understood its potential, the target business outgrew the commercial printing operation. You must stay aware of opportunities that will help your company grow and be more successful.

Put time aside from your normal routine to go through the following list:

1. **Strengths:** Service, special feature or benefit that your product offers

2. **Weaknesses:** limited financial resources, reputation, accounting system

3. **Opportunities:** Increase demands from a new market, new technology, and improved quality

4. **Threats:** New competitors, down turn in the economy, cheaper versions of product or service

Now with all this knowledge you have put together it is time to work on developing a Marketing Strategy. With a good understanding now of your business strengths, weaknesses and external opportunities and threats, you can develop a strategy that plays to your strengths and matches them to emerging opportunities. You can also identify your weaknesses and try to minimize them.

The next step is to draw up a detailed marketing plan that sets out the specific actions to put the strategy into practice. Also consider how you can get the most out of your existing customer base. It is usually more economical and quicker than finding new customs. Remember that customers are always looking for customer service improvements, quality, reliability and efficiency.

In closing this chapter here is the check list!!!

1. Know your business   4. Set goals

2. Determine your best market   5. Set a budget

3. Analyze competitors   6. Get to work

UNITY "THE STATE OF BEING ONE"

Many times when I visited a company the first thing they would bring out would be their organization chart. It would be a group of individual boxes indicating each department's responsibilities for the success of the company. It is all well and good for each employee to know their work assignment, but it is more important that they know they have an obligation to the success of the company at large. Many times I have found that segregation leads to production problems like cover up of procedures, poor communication, needless competition and much more. It is best to express, as best you can, that you are one company and every employee is a member of the team and responsible for the company to be successful.

For a company to be successful it must act as one unit. Each operating function must be done as required and on time. In this exercise I am reminded of a time-watch that, we all know, has many moving parts. However, if one part were to miss functioning the watch would stop. The same thing happens on an assembly line or any production process. This is true for assembly lines and also standalone production facilities.

When you think about operating productively, you should consider the complete process. For a company to function profitably, it must function starting with an exemplary management and accounting unit. From there move on to a top of the line marketing and sales force. Then continue with a well-crafted production and distribution department. Anyone of these operations not functioning properly can stop progress and create losses. It is important to keep in mind that there are no unimportant jobs in a productive and profitable company.

{The End}

Welcome to the Curry family. Got an idea for a book? Contact Curry Brothers Marketing and Publishing Group, LLC. We are not satisfied until your publishing dreams come true. We specialize in all genres of books, especially religion, leadership, family history, poetry, and children's literature. There is an African Proverb that confirms, *"When an elder dies, a library closes."* We advise, be careful who tells your family history. Are their values your family's values? Our staff will navigate you through the entire publishing process, and we take pride in going the extra mile by exceeding your publishing goals.

Improving the world one book at a time!

Curry Brothers Books, LLC
PO Box 247
Haymarket, VA 20168
(719) 466-7518 & (615) 347-9124
Visit us at www.currybrotherspublishing.com

CURRY BROS.
MARKETING + PUBLISHING GROUP

www.ingramcontent.com/pod-product-compliance
Lightning Source LLC
Chambersburg PA
CBHW060358130626
46553CB00003B/1284